Redneck Classic

the best of

Jeff Foxworthy

Illustrations by David Boyd

LONGSTREET PRESS
Atlanta, Georgia

DEDICATION

To J. P., for bringing out the
best in this Redneck. Thank You.
—J. F.

Published by LONGSTREET PRESS, INC.,
a subsidiary of Cox Newspapers,
a subsidiary of Cox Enterprises, Inc.
2140 Newmarket Parkway
Suite 122
Marietta, Georgia 30067

Copyright © 1995 by Jeff Foxworthy

Printed in the United States of America

10th printing, 1998

Library of Congress Catalog Number 95-77243

ISBN: 1-56352-228-4

Jacket design by Neil Hollingsworth
Book design by Jill Dible
The text was set by Laura McDonald

**Jeff Foxworthy's humor also is available on audio tapes and
compact discs from Warner Bros.**

 You Might Be A
Redneck If . . .

 Games
Rednecks
Play

The True, Behind-the-Scenes, Honest-to-God, Embarrassing Story About *How You Might Be A Redneck If . . .* Became a Book

BY STOOP NAGEL*
(*NOT MY REAL NAME, BUT IT FITS)

Jeff Foxworthy's career as a best-selling author began in the most redneck of ways — he was headed for the john and didn't have anything to read.

In desperation he grabbed a week-old newspaper and settled onto every redneck's favorite reading chair. As he scanned the newspaper for announcements of upcoming tractor pulls, his eyes fell on a story about book publishing in the South. More specifically, they fell on a picture of me sitting like a toad behind my cluttered desk at Longstreet Press in Atlanta.

Jeff was a fast-rising stand-up comic, having recently jumped from the rungs of IBM's corporate ladder to center stage at many of the country's leading comedy clubs. Part of his routine was a series of one-liners that identified rednecks — those fun-loving, hard-living Americans whose "family tree does not fork," as Jeff often said. The redneck material had worked so well on stage that Jeff wondered if it might work in written form. That's about the time he saw my picture in the newspaper and told his agent to send me some of the jokes.

A couple of weeks later we met in my office. I loved the redneck material and, like Jeff, thought it might work as well on paper as it did on stage. But more than that, I wanted to find out how he knew so much about my family, on whom he had obviously based the redneck jokes.

I asked the clean-cut comic with a slight accent to tell me about his job. "Welllll," he said for approximately twenty seconds, "I'm on the road 300 nights a year playing comedy clubs. The last show usually ends about 1 a.m., and then about 7 the next morning I have to be on the local radio for an hour to promote that night's show."

Just down the hall I had two employees (called publicists) whose professional mission in life was to get authors on the radio, or television, or in the newspaper to flog their books. And if those authors left their houses in said pursuit, they expected their publisher to pay for it ("ten cents a mile and all the Moon Pies you can eat"). But here, sitting in front of me, was a fellow who traveled all over the country on his own nickel and who *had* to be on the radio every day. Being an astute businessman, I immediately saw possibilities. Those redneck jokes were getting funnier by the minute.

"I think we can work something out," I said, "but there is one issue I want to discuss with you." As a proponent of regional pride ("American by Birth, Southern by the Grace of God"), I was a little concerned about the use of the term *redneck*. In the mouths and minds of some Americans of the Northern persuasion, for example, it is occasionally used as a term of derision, as in, "This redneck moron in a pick-up truck with tires the size of Rhode Island nearly forced me off the turnpike. Would you like a soda pop and a frank?" So I suggested to Jeff that maybe we would be best served (and less ridiculed) by naming the book *You Might Be a Bubba If....*

Jeff squinted a bit and then said, "Wellllll, I use this material every night in front of a live audience, and no one has ever been bothered by it. You may not realize it, but there are honest-to-God rednecks all over this country." Then he told me about the bowling alley in Detroit that had valet parking.

To my eternal credit, I yielded to his wisdom. The book would be called *You Might Be a Redneck If....*

Next we tackled the thorny business side of publishing — the issues of advances and royalties. "Since we're not sure how this is going to work," I said, posturing a bit, "how about an advance of $1,500?" For a moment, I knew by the look in Jeff's eyes that he was wondering where he was going to come up with that much money, so I added, "We'll pay *you* that amount against royalties on future sales."

"Wellllll," he said, "just how many copies do you think we might sell?"

Being an experienced professional with keen insight into the publishing business, I gave him my best estimate: "I'll be happy if we sell 10,000 copies," I said. (For the record, the number of *You Might Be a Redneck If...* books, shirts, CDs, hats, post cards, etc., sold so far is counted in the *millions.* Jeff was right — there are rednecks everywhere!)

We agreed that illustrations would be a nice addition to the book, so I suggested a cartoonist whose style I thought was a good fit. David Boyd of Newnan, Georgia, later met with Jeff and me to discuss the drawings. When a deal was struck, Boyd said to Jeff, "I have just one question before I leave: How do you know so much about my family?"

So that's the story, the true story, of how Jeff Foxworthy first got published. I may have been bad wrong in my sales projections, but at least I was smart enough to recognize incredible talent when it "slapped me upside the head," as one of Jeff's rednecks might say. God bless 'em. And long may they reproduce (outside the family).

— The Editor

Redneck Classic

the best of
Jeff Foxworthy

You've ever shot anyone for looking at you.

You think the stock market has a fence around it.

You own a home that is mobile and five cars that aren't.

You go to a party and the punch bowl flushes.

You think the last four words of the National Anthem are, "Gentlemen, start your engines!"

Somebody hollers "Hoe down!" and your girlfriend hits the floor.

Any of your children were conceived in a car wash.

You've ever held up someone with a caulk gun.

Your wife has ever said, "Come move this transmission so I can take a bath."

Your grandmother has ever been asked to leave a bingo game because of her language.

You take your dog for a walk and you both use the same tree at the corner.

Your kids take a siphon hose to "Show and Tell."

The most common phrase heard in your house is, "Somebody go jiggle the handle."

You've ever been kicked out of the zoo for heckling the monkeys.

You Might Be A Redneck If . . .

You think a subdivision is part of a math problem.

Your good deed for the month was hiding
your brother for a few days.

You think "taking out the trash" means taking
your in-laws to a movie.

The dog catcher calls for a back-up unit when
visiting your house.

Your grandmother knows how to correctly execute the "sleeper hold."

You pick your teeth from a catalog.

You can't take a nap without at least one hand tucked inside your pants.

You think "Long John Silver" is formal underwear.

You can entertain yourself for more than an hour with a fly swatter.

Your property has been mistaken for
a recycling center.

You've ever been to the ear, nose and throat
doctor to have your finger removed.

You've ever plucked a nose hair with a pair of pliers.

You think Liberation was that funny dressed
guy who played the piano.

You use a fishing license as a form of I.D.

You've ever been accused of lying through your tooth.

You refer to your wife and mother-in-law
as "dual air bags."

On stag night, you take a real deer.

You've ever
stolen toilet
paper.

There is more oil in your baseball cap than in your car.

You think a hot tub is a stolen bathroom fixture.

There's an expired license plate hanging on
your living room wall.

Your wife has
ever burned out
an electric razor.

You Might Be A Redneck If . . .

You think "cur" is a breed of dog.

✧

Your best shoes have numbers on the heels.

✧

Taking a dip has nothing to do with water.

✧

You take a fishing pole into Sea World.

✧

Your toilet paper has page numbers on it.

✧

You list your parole officer as a reference.

Your screen door has no screen.

There are more fish on your walls than pictures.

✧

You think a turtleneck is a key ingredient to soup.

✧

You think the French Riviera is a foreign car.

You've been on TV more than once describing what the tornado sounded like.

Truckers tell your wife to watch her language.

The family business requires a lookout.

When packing for vacation, your biggest decision is whether to use paper or plastic.

You have to curl the sides of your cowboy hat
so your wife can ride in the truck, too.

You Might Be A Redneck If . . .

You think the phrase "chicken out" means one of your pets has escaped.

You have to take the entire day off work to get your teeth cleaned.

You've ever been pumping gas and another customer asks you to check his oil.

You've ever been arrested for relieving yourself in an ice machine.

You've ever run down a bowling lane and slid into the pins.

You consider dating second cousins as "playing the field."

You go to your sister's wedding just to kiss the bride.

You think the Bud Bowl is real.

You Might Be A Redneck If . . .

You have lots of hubcaps on your house
but none on your car.

You've ever eaten out of a minnow bucket.

Your bra size is higher than your S.A.T. score.

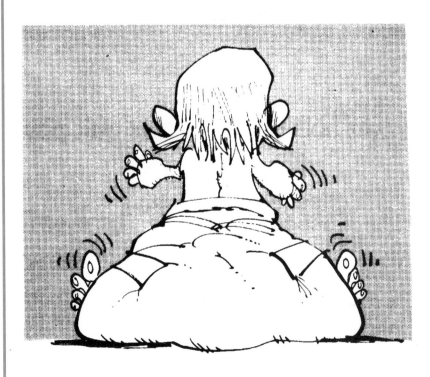

You think "six to ten pounds" on the side of the Pampers box means how much the diaper will hold.

You Might Be A Redneck If . . .

You've ever hollered, "You kids quit playing
on that sheet metal!"

✧

You can name the entire cast of
"The Dukes of Hazzard" but not your congressman.

✧

You think the Battle of the Bulge is an argument
between your wife and your mother.

✧

You hold a frog and it worries about getting warts.

✧

You think safe sex is when the participants
are married to each other.

You paint your car with house paint.

You go fishing with a generator and copper wire.

You can drink beer through your nose.

Your dog goes "oink!"

You Might Be A Redneck If . . .

You've ever committed a crime with a lawn mower.

Your family talks just like professional wrestlers.

You think espresso means eight items or less.

You think the Nutcracker is something you did off the high dive.

Your mailbox is
made out of old
auto parts.

You Might Be A Redneck If . . .

Your hood ornament used to be a
bowling trophy.

✧

You own half of a pick-up truck.

✧

You know how to milk a goat.

✧

You have to check your shirt to spell your name.

✧

A full moon reminds you of your
mother-in-law pulling weeds.

You stare at a can of frozen orange juice
because it says "concentrate."

You have a black eye and a hickey
at the same time.

Your kids
have a
three-day-old
Kool-Aid
mustache.

You think the Yellow Pages has something
to do with training a puppy.

Your new sofa was on a curb in another
part of town yesterday.

You bring a bar
of soap to a
public pool.

You Might Be A Redneck If . . .

You've ever given yourself a social disease.

✧

All your relatives would have to die to wipe out illiteracy.

✧

Your two-year-old has more teeth than you do.

✧

You won't go to the family Christmas party unarmed.

✧

Your dog passes gas and you claim it.

You Might Be A Redneck If . . .

Your trim your beard and find a french fry.

Your satellite dish has more square footage
than your house.

You thought Ned Beatty was sexy in *Deliverance*.

Your TV gets 512 channels, but you go
outside to use the bathroom.

Your wife would rather fish off a bridge
than shop for clothes.

You see a sign that says "Just say no to crack!" and it reminds you to pull up your jeans.

There are tobacco stains down the side of your school bus.

You made jewelry out of your gallstones.

You ever applied for a job while wearing a stocking cap.

Everyone in your family is an Elvis impersonator.

Your car burns more oil than gas.

You've ever walked through a drive-thru window.

You've ever used pantyhose as a coffee filter.

You Might Be A Redneck If . . .

You offer to give somebody the shirt off your back and they don't want it.

✧

Your wife has a set of earrings that you use as a fishing lure.

✧

Neither you nor your husband's job requires you to wear a shirt to work.

✧

You refer to hot sex as relative humidity.

✧

You missed your high school graduation because your kids were sick.

Your belt
buckle is
bigger than
your head.

You Might Be A Redneck If . . .

You think *Roe v. Wade* deals with boat ownership.

✧

Your car breaks down on the side of the road and you never go back to get it.

✧

You've ever stood outside a bathroom and heckled someone inside.

✧

Your riding lawn mower has cup holders.

✧

You think the Super Bowl is a top-of-the-line bathroom fixture.

Your toothbrush has been in the family for generations.

✦

You have to wash your hands before
going to the bathroom.

✦

There are antlers nailed to the outside of your house.

You've ever asked a widow for her phone
number at the funeral home.

**You think toilet water
is exactly that.**

You've ever left Santa a PBR and a Slim Jim.

Your parrot can say, "Open up, it's the police!"

You think "recycling" means going home from work.

You Might Be A Redneck If . . .

You've ever been the first person in or the last person out of a video arcade.

You wore curlers to your wedding so you would look nice at the reception.

Your veterinarian is also a taxidermist.

You shave your legs with your husband's fishing knife.

You make your wife ride in the back of the truck so the dog won't get sick.

Your first pet was a chicken.

Your chili's secret ingredient comes from the bait shop.

Turning on your lights involves pulling a string.

You wet the bed and four other people immediately know it.

You Might Be A Redneck If . . .

You have a refrigerator just for beer.

Your lawn furniture used to be your
living room furniture.

Any of your children are the result of a conjugal visit.

Your dog
can smoke a
cigarette.

You Might Be A Redneck If . . .

You come back from the dump with more than you took.

✧

Coworkers start a petition over your coffee cup.

✧

You've ever backed down an exit ramp.

✧

You've ever appeared on television not wearing a shirt.

✧

You have a hook in your shower to
hang your hat on.

✧

You've ever eaten so much that your bra hurt you.

You Might Be A Redneck If . . .

The trunk of your car is tied down and
you're not hauling anything.

✧

Your flashlight holds more than four batteries.

✧

Your truck can pass over a 55-gallon drum
without touching it.

✧

Your Christmas tree has a deer stand in it.

✧

You refer to the fifth grade as "my senior year."

✧

You have a tattoo that says, "Born to bag groceries."

The last photos of your mama were taken from the front and the side.

STIFFSOCK COUNTY SHERIFF DEPT.
OA 649-442-9884
JULY 3, 1989

STIFFSOCK COUNTY SHERIFF DEPT.
OA 649-442-9884
JULY 3, 1989

Your wife owns a camouflage nightie.

Your muffler is held on by a coat hanger.

You have orange road cones in your living room.

You Might Be A Redneck If . . .

There is a ham hanging from your front porch.

You can take your bra off while driving.

You walk into a restaurant with a toothpick in your mouth.

The rear window of your truck or van is a picture.

42

You Might Be A Redneck If . . .

You've given away more free puppies than
the animal shelter.

You have to mow your driveway.

You've ever used lard in bed.

Going to the bathroom in the middle of the night requires shoes and a flashlight.

You Might Be A Redneck If . . .

You own Patsy Cline salt and pepper shakers.

You think a house warming is something the KKK does.

The highlight of your family reunion was your sister's nude dancing debut.

Your high school annual is now a mug shot book for the police department.

You consider a six pack of beer and a bug-zapper quality entertainment.

You prefer to walk the excess length off your jeans rather than hem them.

You pick your nose in line at the bank.

You have a tennis ball on your antenna.

Someone asks
to see your I.D.
and you show
them your belt
buckle.

You Might Be A Redneck If . . .

You've ever worn cowboy boots with Bermuda shorts.

Anything outside the Lower 48 is "overseas."

You own all the components of soap on a
rope except the soap.

Every car you've ever owned was wrecked.

Your car has never had a full tank of gas.

Your mother does not remove the Marlboro from her lips before telling the state patrolman to kiss her ass.

Your wife carries a can of Vienna sausage in her purse.

Directions to your house include "turn off the paved road."

You know how many bales of hay your car can hold.

You honest-to-God think women are turned on by animal noises and seductive tongue gestures.

You don't think baseball players spit and scratch too much.

Your
pocketknife
often doubles
as a toothpick.

Hail hits your house and you have to take it to the body shop for an estimate.

Your dog has a litter of puppies on the living room floor and nobody notices.

Your dog and your wallet are both on a chain.

Your family
tree does not
fork.

You Might Be A Redneck If . . .

You did not put the pink plastic flamingos
in your front yard as a joke.

You've ever had hot flashes at a cattle auction.

You've ever borrowed chewing tobacco
from your wife.

You rip a loud one and blame your date.

You have a rag for a gas cap.

The dog can't watch you eat without gagging.

You have to dress up the kids to go to Kmart.

You have a Hefty Bag for a passenger-side window.

Your wife's hairdo
has ever ruined a
ceiling fan.

You ever "hit on" somebody in a V.D. clinic.

Your brother-in-law is also your uncle.

Every workday ends with the same argument about who gets to ride in the cab of the truck.

You've ever ridden all the way to Florida with your bare feet hanging out the car window.

You've ever been too drunk to fish.

All your four-letter words are two syllables.

You view the upcoming family reunion as a chance to meet women.

Your house doesn't have curtains but your truck does.

Your front porch collapses and kills more than three dogs.

You've ever heard a sheep bleat and had romantic thoughts.

You wonder how service stations keep their bathrooms so clean.

You think "The dishwasher is broke" means
your wife has no money.

You consider your license plate "personalized"
because your father made it.

**Your mother keeps a spit cup on
the ironing board.**

You Might Be A Redneck If . . .

You've ever written Richard Petty's name
on a presidential ballot.

You are allowed to bring your dog to work.

You think the
Styrofoam
cooler is the
greatest
invention of
all time.

You Might Be A Redneck If . . .

You've ever had to haul a can of paint
to the top of a water tower to
defend your sister's honor.

✧

You own a homemade pair of lizard skin boots.

✧

You can field dress a deer but can't
change a diaper.

✧

You play pin-the-tail-on-the-donkey and
get four teeth kicked out.

You've ever had sex in a satellite dish.

You Might Be A Redneck If . . .

. . . you can smoke a cigarette to the end without knocking off the ash.

. . . you've ever lost a tooth opening a beer bottle.

. . . there are more than 10
lawsuits currently
pending against
your dog.

. . . you think Old Yeller
is a movie about your
brother's tooth.

. . . you've ever been caught in a crossfire at a family reunion.

. . . the major color of your automobile is Bondo.

. . . you have ever worn cowboy boots with Bermuda shorts.

. . . your dentist dreads seeing you more than you dread seeing him.

. . . your Fourth of July cookout has ever been ruined because your daddy got drunk and burned the Spam.

. . . you've ever tuned up your car in front of an auto parts store.

. . . the pink flamingo in your front yard has buckshot holes in it.

. . . your mama taught you how to flip a cigarette.

. . . you have an above ground swimming pool that you fish out of.

. . . strangers knock on your door mistakenly thinking you're having a yard sale.

. . . you strip naked to the waist to eat barbecue.

. . . you have ever given your mama jumper cables for Mother's Day.

. . . strangers mistakenly think your children are already dressed for "trick or treat."

. . . like the
Pilgrims of old,
you brought your own kill to
the Thanksgiving table.

You Might Be A Redneck If . . .

. . . you have an old commode somewhere in your front yard with flowers growing in it.

. . . you've ever ridden on a luggage rack.

73

. . . your nativity scene has people wearing camouflage.

. . . your outdoor Christmas decoration has a misspelled word.

. . . you drove to elementary school.

. . . there's a motor hanging from a tree any- where in your yard.

You Might Be A Redneck If . . .

. . . you have ever taken an inner tube up a ski lift.

Original Drawings by *Jofworthy*

During the last ten years, I've spent more time in airports than a tribe of Hare Krishnas. To pass the time while waiting for late flights, I often sketch some of the faces I see coming and going. Some-times I draw a face and then think of an appropriate line for it; other times the line comes first and then the matching face appears. Like rednecks, humor is all around us . . . if we'll just look.

— J.F.

Pete teased the children by pretending he was going to sneeze.

For Ernie, it was a secluded trout stream
and Gina's garter belt.

**Roy contemplated throwing it all away
and becoming a dancer.**

Through the years Stumpy Lynch became somewhat of an expert with fireworks.

Ernest worried that Wanda knew he wore a toupeé.

Frank now knew, Lou had the old maid.

If you bought Leonard a cup of coffee,
he'd tell you about his alien abduction.

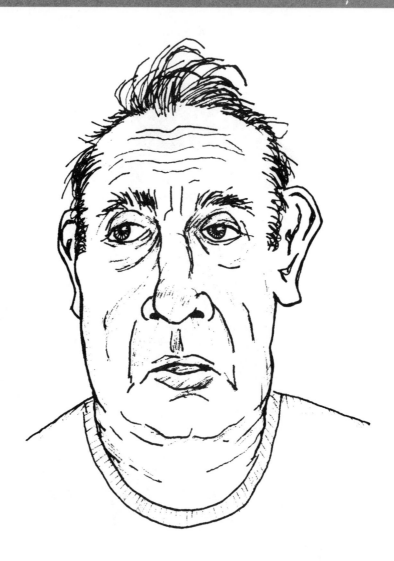

Wade's announcement that the burritos weren't "sitting well" sent family members running to make other sleeping arrangements.

**Stanley tries to break open the 0-0 tie
at the C.P.A. softball game.**

Clete helps the Campbells get their cat out of a tree.

Most guys hated the occasional jolt of electricity, not Art Winkleman.

Roland plays Jeopardy.

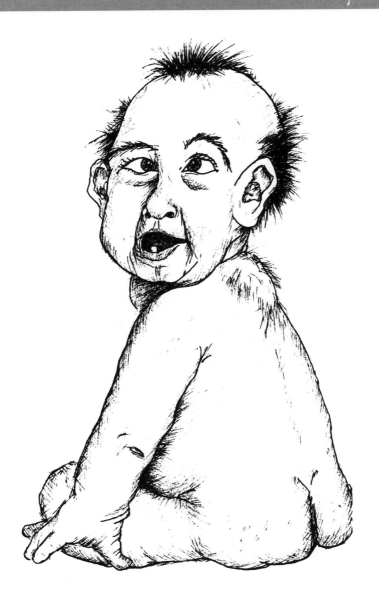

**There were ugly babies . . .
then there was the Horton kid.**

Ladies club craft champion Irene Moore and her hand-painted Richard Nixon yellow squash.

You're not a kid anymore

One evening not long ago, while watering the lawn, I yelled at someone for driving down our street too fast. As soon as I realized what I had done, I dropped the hose and began to shake. I sounded just like my dad! I'm getting old!

How did this happen? Where did the years go? I used to be hip, but lately the only reason I'm up past midnight is indigestion. Last week I caught myself reading the obituaries, and one morning when I left the house I took along an umbrella just because it was cloudy.

Age can sneak up on you before you know it, so here are some ways to spot it.

— J.F.

You're asleep, but others worry that you're dead.

You can live without sex but not without your glasses.

Your back goes out more than you do.

You quit trying to hold your stomach in, no matter who walks into the room.

You buy a compass for the dash of your car.

You are proud of your lawn mower.

Your best friend is dating someone half his age...
and isn't breaking any laws.

You call Olan Mills before they call you.

Your arms
are almost
too short to
read the
newspaper.

You sing along with the elevator music.

You would rather go to work than stay home sick.

You constantly talk about the price of gasoline.

You enjoy
hearing about
other people's
operations.

94

You're not a kid anymore when . . .

You make an appointment to see the dentist.

✧

You no longer think of speed limits as a challenge.

✧

Neighbors borrow your tools.

✧

People call at 9 p.m. and ask,
"Did I wake you?"

✧

You have a dream about prunes.

✧

You answer a question with, "Because I said so!"

You send money to PBS.

You still buy records, and you think a CD
is a certificate of deposit.

The end of
your tie
doesn't come
anywhere
near the top
of your
pants.

You're not a kid anymore when . . .

You take a metal detector to the beach.

You wear black socks with sandals.

You know what the word "equity" means.

Your Chihuahua weighs more than 25 pounds.

You have
more than two
spare pairs of
glasses.

You can't remember the last time you lay
on the floor to watch television.

You name your hot water bottle.

Your ears
are hairier
than your
head.

You're not a kid anymore when . . .

You talk about "good grass," and you're
referring to someone's lawn.

✧

You hope it doesn't snow.

✧

You get into a heated argument about pension plans.

✧

You start believing that you really did walk five
miles to school barefoot and in the snow.

✧

You can go bowling without drinking.

✧

You got cable TV just for the weather channel.

Your bell-bottoms are belled at both ends.

You can quickly find anything in your garage.

You have a party and the neighbors don't even realize it.

You think about Walter Cronkite at least once a day.

All the pictures on your walls are framed.

You are obsessed with the thermostat.

There are no cinderblock and board
bookcases in your house.

Someone
sees you
naked and
screams.

You tell the barber to comb it over the best he can.

HICK IS CHIC

"Mind your manners!" I bet I heard that phrase a million times when I was growing up. Translated into Mom language, it usually meant something like, "Quit trying to balance that fish stick on your nose!"

I was half grown, however, before I finally realized that the "Social Graces" was not a gospel singing group. About that same time, I also realized that I wasn't embarrassing Mom anymore; I was embarrassing myself. So, as an educational service to my fellow Redneckers, I compiled a guide to etiquette for the grossly unsophisticated, and I called it *HICK IS CHIC*.

— J.F.

HICK IS CHIC / *Personal Hygiene*

EARS:

While **ears** need to be cleaned regularly, this is a job that should be done in private using one's own **truck keys.** (NOTE: Keys must also be cleaned regularly, because ear wax buildup can short-circuit a starter switch.) **Post office keys** are recommended for deep probing.

MANICURES AND PEDICURES:

Sometimes you may find it impossible to chew a **fingernail** evenly. Don't panic. Household scissors or a sharp steak knife can usually handle the task. **Toenails,** however, present a tougher problem, and a strong wood file or bolt-cutters often provide the answer. Remember to always put nail clippings in their proper place — the ashtray.

• **Dirt and grease** under nails is a social no-no, as they tend to detract from a woman's jewelry and alter the tastes of finger foods.

• **Corns and calluses** can be removed using a common potato peeler. Remember never to cut against the grain.

HAIR CARE:

(For Men) Contrary to popular belief, **dandruff** is not an incurable disease. And despite what the guys around the gas pump say, **shampooing** regularly is not the leading cause of homosexuality. If you can't afford store-bought hair tonic, **brake fluid** not only holds the hair in place but also adds a dark, Elvis-like sheen to the scalp.

(For Women) **Sponge rollers** (pink or green) are a beauty tool no woman should be without. Rolling them too tight, however, can result in nasty headaches and cause the eyes to dry out. While a **tall hive of hair** is the current rage, it can be an open invitation to bees and hornets. A 50/50 mixture of Black Flag and hairspray can prove to be a girl's best summertime friend.

NOSE HAIR:

Plucking these unwanted devils one at a time will work, but a **cigarette lighter** and a small tolerance for pain can accomplish the same goal and save hours.

MAKE-UP:

Good make-up, like a good paint job, requires a clean surface and a **primer coat**. Fortunately, most bars are pretty dark, and beer can be counted on to blur the vision of prospects. In most cases, an **extra Bud** can be just as effective as extra blush.

BRUSHING & FLOSSING:

Scientists have proven that the use of a **toothbrush** (and toothpaste when available) can help people keep their teeth into their thirties and even beyond. **Dental floss,** the modern equivalent of broom straw, is also helpful. A lightweight monofilament fishing line works just as well, but I do recommend removing all **lures** from the line before flossing.

JEWELRY:

"It looks pretty but it turns my **neck green**!" This is a common complaint about 3K gold. If this is a problem for you, try other **precious metals** such as tin or aluminum.

GLOVES:

A woman should always wear gloves with a full-length evening gown, as well as when she is **handling rope** or operating heavy machinery. Do not wear **rubber gloves** in public, even if they don't match your dress.

CLOTHING:

In summertime, nothing accentuates a nice **shoulder tattoo** like a sundress. And here's how to make that listless butterfly come alive: When you go to the river to sunbathe, cover the tattoo with some of your date's used **chewing tobacco**. The rest of your skin will turn a bright red when **sunburned**, but the tattoo will remain creamy white. The effect can be startling, making the butterfly appear to be in flight.

As for **bathing suits**, the expression "If you've got it, flaunt it!" does *not* apply to hips. A good rule of thumb is three square feet of fabric for every 100 pounds. While flannel may feel good against your skin, avoid **flannel** bathing suits; they tend to sag even when you don't.

Finally, **hip waders** are not considered dress pants.

HICK IS CHIC / *Fashion for Men*

This subject can be summarized in a single phrase: **No collar, no tie**.

ORDERING:

When dining out, it is recommended that the man order for his female companion. Nothing can be more **embarrassing** than having to counter your date's, "I think I'll have the deluxe platter," with, "Think again." Also, as a matter of pure convenience, it is easier for the man to order since he is usually driving and is **closer to the speaker**.

WINE:

In fancy restaurants, wine bottles usually come sealed with a **cork** instead of a screw-on cap. Consider this a bonus and pocket the cork for a future fishing trip. It is the responsibility of the person who orders the wine to taste it before serving it to others (**gargling** is frowned upon). If the wine is bad, do not spit it out and yell, "Somebody forgot to **wash their feet** before they stomped those grapes!"

THE FOOD:

Once the food is served, try to avoid telling any stories about **car wrecks, operations, or sick pets.** Nothing ruins a good meal quicker than someone getting sick or sentimental at the table. Also, while perfectly okay at home, remember that it is considered crass when dining out to ask, "Are you gonna eat the rest of that **meatloaf**?" Especially if you don't know the person.

COMMON QUESTIONS:

Q: When is it proper to be seated?

A: After the hostess is seated, or whenever you feel gas coming on.

Q: Is it okay to dip your bread in gravy?

A: Only if the gravy is on your own clothes.

Q: Is it proper to reach across the table?

A: Yes, just as in shooting pool, as long as you keep one foot on the floor.

Sometimes you may find yourself in certain social settings where you don't know anyone. It can be extremely awkward trying to converse with strangers, so here are some openers guaranteed to break the ice:

- How much do you want for that refrigerator on the front porch?

- Is that an extra-firm mattress on top of your car?

- I bought some pearls just like those at a yard sale last weekend.

- Do I have anything stuck in my teeth?

- Whose feet stink?

- How long have you had that thing on your nose?

- Let's step out on the porch where the flies ain't so bad.

• Make your guests feel at home. Let them adjust the rabbit ears on the TV, and make the dog give up the couch.

• Take the trash out a couple of days before guests arrive. It is difficult to be witty when your nose burns.

• Do not continue ironing after guests arrive.

• Be careful about serving leftovers. A good rule of thumb is, "If the dogs won't eat it, company probably won't either."

• If your guests overstay their welcome, it may be necesssary to give them hints that it's time to leave. I suggest a gentle reminder such as, "Y'all are either going to have to leave or chip in on the rent."

• Even if a guest is dominating the conversation, refrain from saying, "How 'bout putting some teeth in that hole."

• A centerpiece for the table should never be anything prepared by a taxidermist.

• Do not allow the dog to eat off the table . . . no matter how good his manners are.

• Cover those nasty burn holes in the carpet with strategically placed old newspapers.

• Remember to reserve the VFW far in advance, and avoid Saturdays, since that's square dancing night.

• When going through the receiving line, it is proper to say something nice to the bride, such as, "Your baby is real cute."

• If someone asks where the bride is registered, do *not* answer, "The American Kennel Club."

• Livestock is usually a poor choice for a wedding gift.

• Kissing the bride for more than five seconds (or slipping her the tongue) may get you cut.

• When throwing rice at the bride and groom, use uncooked rice and toss it underhanded.

• If the wedding is cancelled, the girl should return the ring. If her brother has already killed the ex-groom, the ring should be returned to his next of kin.

Here's another valuable hint: a bridal veil made of window screen is not only cost effective but also a proven fly deterrent.

OTHER WEDDING QUESTIONS:

Q: Is it all right to bring a date to a wedding?
A: Not if you are the groom.

Q: How many showers is the bride supposed to have?
A: At least one within a week of the wedding.

Q: How many bridal attendants should the bride have?
A: One for each of her kids.

• When traveling with your family, try to keep their "moon-ing" of other drivers to a minimum.

• Dim your headlights for approaching vehicles, even if the gun is loaded and the deer is in sight.

• When approaching a four-way stop, remember that the vehicle with the largest tires always has the right of way.

• Never tow another car using pantyhose and duct tape.

• When sending your wife down the road with a gas can, it is impolite to ask her to bring back beer.

• Never relieve yourself from a moving vehicle, especially when driving.

• When traveling with a mattress on top of the car, do *not* allow others to take a nap on it.

• Never fish from a moving vehicle.

• Remember that the median is not a passing lane.

• Rugs need to be occasionally beaten, not just threatened.

• Never set off a flea bomb in someone else's home without asking first.

• When receiving visitors in the hospital, you don't *have* to show your scar. Not everyone is fascinated by a vasectomy.

• When giving birth, have a relative call your school so you won't be charged with an unexplained absence.

• Never go up to a stranger on the beach and ask if you can get that pimple on his back.

• Always offer to bait your date's hook, especially on the first date.

• If your dog falls in love with a guest's leg, have the decency to leave them alone for a few minutes.

• When viewing the deceased at a funeral home, never say, "He looks so natural. Like he just got drunk and passed out."

• If you need to vacuum the bed, it's time to change the sheets.

• Tip the valet extra if he has to push or jump-start your car.

• At movie theaters, refrain from talking to characters on the screen. Tests have shown that they can't hear you.

Games Rednecks Play

When Atlanta, Georgia, was selected as the site for the 1996 Olympic Games — which marks the 100th anniversary of the modern-day games — a lot of highbrows were raised. Why Atlanta, they questioned, instead of Athens, Greece, where the games supposedly originated?

But to anyone who knows a speck of history, locating the centennial Games in the South — a breeding ground for Rednecks — made perfect sense. As long as there have been homemade whiskey and a little free time, Rednecks have always been world leaders at creating fun and games. They can make a game out of anything — from hitting mailboxes with a baseball bat to hunting deer with a Jeep. And as every Redneck will attest, it's not whether you win or lose, it's whether or not you'll have a good story to tell later on. So kick off your shoes, prop up your feet, get yourself something cold to drink, and enjoy this sampling of *Games Rednecks Play*.

Let the games begin! — J.F.

GAMES REDNECKS PLAY / *Water Sports*

Sculling — A precision sport. Just the right touch can produce a few hours of peace and quiet, but too much force can result in a murder rap.

Breast Stroke — Rarely witnessed but often talked about. Most stories open with the words, "This ol' gal...."

Platform Diving — A good set of rear shocks with a rock behind the wheel and you're in business. The first diver must be a man of honor, as subsequent divers will invariably ask, "How deep is it?"

Rowing — Not the most popular sport because most Rednecks agree that, "If you can't afford a motor, you can't afford a boat." A good rowing team, however, can pull a skier.

Skipping Rocks — The oldest and most traditional of all the Redneck games. The heavyweight division is most popular, as contestants try to skip bricks.

Flinging — Originated by an ancient Redneck trying to clean his yard. A great fling is not only a beautiful thing to watch, but often it is accompanied by the exciting sound of something breaking.

Long Jump — This sport is a Redneck favorite, since they all own numerous sets of jumper cables and all their vehicles have dead or dying batteries.

Modern Pentathlon — The winner is the one who gets furthest through the entire *Penthouse* magazine library without having to excuse himself.

4 X 4 Relay — Remember, always downshift when passing the baton.

2 X 4 Relay — Originated at night on construction sites by people looking to enlarge their homes at low-budget prices.

Hammer Throw — A good hammer throw is almost always immediately preceded by a smashed thumb and a shouted expletive. Roofers tend to dominate this game.

Mare-a-thon — Contestants get drunk and see who can stay on a horse the longest. Great champions always have a butt rash.

Field Hockey — Who can run the farthest through a cow pasture without stepping in "you know what"? A really exciting game when played at night with flashlights.

Broad Jump — Mercy upon those who fall short. It ain't pretty.

Hat Shooting — A competition between two Rednecks, usually preceded by some serious drinking. Going first is a *big* advantage, since the second contestant is sometimes too dead to take his turn.

Tracking — We're not talking about anything as sissy as following a blood trail. A good tracker can trail a grasshopper down the interstate. A favorite put-down in this sport is, "You couldn't track a slug across a sheet of glass."

Hog Calling — The good ones can bring a sow into Times Square using only their voice. The *great* ones are often victims of sexual assault by live pork.

Bush-Hogging for Distance — Put her in drive and hold on tight. A sharp blade and a blatant disregard for personal property are essential to this game.

Engine Rebuilding — Rules state that cars must remain on your property at all times. Not a sport for the easily bored spectator, as Rednecks often take a lifetime to rebuild an engine.

Mooning — Whether it's pressed ham against a passenger-side window or a full hang from the rear of a truck, few things match the thrill of making someone else look at your naked rear-end when they're not expecting it.

Shopping Cart Racing — The bag boys' sport of choice. Join them for a death ride as these interlocked, wobble-wheeled locomotives without steering or brakes speed back to the cart corral.

Creeper Luge — Originated after work on Fridays when business was slow at the Hilltop Garage. This sport can be really exciting when there's a busy intersection at the bottom of the hill.

Haulin' — Grab your wife, kids, and dogs, and we're off to the dump. Contestants must stop and pick up anything of value they spot along the way.

Spitting for Distance — Strong neck muscles, bad sinuses, and a good wind are necessary to be a champion. Judges for this event are hard to find, even though they are given a laundry allowance.

Peeing for Distance — A male dominated sport, although "Wild Rose" McGee can be a contender if she's had enough to drink. Divisions include parking lot, redwood deck, and hotel balcony.

Fencing — If there's one thing Rednecks know about, it's fences. Compulsory elements include used appliances, old pallets, sheet metal, car doors, and bailing wire.

Homemade Tattoos — The sport which begat the phrase, "An idle mind is the devil's workshop." This event is particularly difficult for Rednecks, since judges deduct points for incorrect spellings.

"Mercy!" — Restricted to females 45 and older. Contestants dab away tears, wring their hands, and moan, "Mercy!" for hours. This event was originated by two middle-aged women telling each other about their "female problems."

Weightlifting — What better way to prove one's self-worth than by picking up something heavy? Hemorrhoids and hernias are a champion's constant companions.